W9-ATO-048

WITHDRAWN

2/17

Get to Work with Science and Technology

Creating Visual Effects for Movies as a

CGI Artist

by Ruth Owen

Consultant:

Ian Failes

VFX and animation journalist and consultant

Ruby Tuesday Books

Published in 2017 by Ruby Tuesday Books Ltd.

Editor: Mark J. Sachner
Designers: Tammy West and Emma Randall
Production: John Lingham

Photo Credits:
Alamy: 7, 8–9, 10, 11 (bottom), 13 (bottom), 17 (bottom), 20–21, 24–25, 27, 29; The Kobal Collection: 4–5, 11 (top), 14, 22–23, 26; Shutterstock: Cover, 12, 13 (top), 15, 16, 17 (top), 19, 28, 30; Wikipedia Creative Commons: 6, 18.

Library of Congress Control Number: 2016907602

ISBN 978-1-910549-89-6

Printed and published in the United States of America

For further information including rights and permissions requests, please contact our Customer Service Department at 877-337-8577.

Contents

A New Kind of Jungle

In a dark movie theater, the audience falls silent and gets ready to enjoy *The Jungle Book*.

They hold back tears as Mowgli says goodbye to Raksha, his wolf mother. They laugh as the little boy and his bear buddy Baloo get into trouble. Some people cover their eyes in terror as Mowgli does battle with the vengeful tiger, Shere Khan. It's hard to believe that the only real thing on the screen is the young actor Neel Sethi.

The movie's jungle setting and the 70 different species of animals that appear are **CGI (computer-generated imagery)**. They only exist because of the skills and creativity of a team of CGI artists!

Mowgli (Neel Sethi) and Raksha say goodbye.

The millions of hairs on Baloo the bear's body all had to move and catch the light realistically.

The Jungle Book is a live-action/ CGI film. This means it combines human actors with computer-generated characters and action.

Making Movie Magic

Today, computer-generated imagery can bring to life the ideas of even the most imaginative movie director. But how did **visual effects (VFX)** experts create dramatic effects in the past?

One way was to build miniature models and then bring them to life using a type of **animation** called stop-motion animation. In this technique, a model is photographed. Then it is moved a tiny amount and photographed again. When the series of photographs, or **frames**, are shown together at high speed, the model appears to be moving.

In the 1933 movie *King Kong*, the giant ape was actually a model just 18 inches (46 cm) high. The model ape's hair was made from rabbit fur.

The skeleton battle scene from *Jason and the Argonauts*.

Stop-motion **animator** Ray Harryhausen produced a famous battle between skeletons and human characters in the 1963 movie *Jason and the Argonauts*. He filmed models of skeletons in stop-motion. Then he combined the animated fight scene with film of human actors.

Ray Harryhausen's skeletons were just a few inches high. He worked on the stop-motion skeleton fight for more than four months. When completed, the battle scene lasted just four minutes.

Computers Go to the Movies

Audiences were wowed by early visual effects. As computers became a part of everyday life, however, movie makers realized they also offered limitless creative possibilities.

One of the first movies to feature CGI was released in 1982. *Tron* is the story of a computer programmer who finds himself transported inside the **software** of a computer system. The movie's 20 minutes of CGI action were created on a computer that had 500 times less memory than one of today's smartphones.

Director Steven Lisberger's movie *Tron* features actor Jeff Bridges in a high-speed race between digital racing bikes called light cycles.

This triceratops in *Jurassic Park* was filmed on a platform. Puppeteers controlled its movements with levers and pulleys from beneath the platform.

In 1993, director Steven Spielberg brought dinosaurs back from extinction in *Jurassic Park*. The movie combined life-size **animatronic** dinosaur models, a man in a dinosaur suit, and around six minutes of sequences created with CGI.

Visual effects expert John Rosengrant played one of *Jurassic Park*'s terrifying, flesh-hungry velociraptors. Wearing a foam rubber suit, he stalked and attacked the movie's human characters.

In order to move like a dinosaur, Rosengrant studied lizards and large birds.

Out of This World

In 1995, director James Cameron began writing a movie that was set on an alien moon named Pandora. Cameron knew exactly what he wanted to create, but the technology to do it had not yet been invented. By 2005, advancements in CGI made it possible for Cameron's vision to come alive. That vision was the **groundbreaking** movie *Avatar*.

The *Avatar* team developed a system called a virtual camera. The actors were filmed running or fighting inside the **studio**. When this action was viewed through the virtual camera, however, the team could see the actors' CGI characters running and fighting inside the CGI world of Pandora.

The magical floating mountain peaks were just one of the incredible Pandoran landscapes.

Avatar's CGI team developed an entire world of new animals, including six-legged, horse-like creatures and giant, flying dragons, such as the Toruk, shown here.

Cameron brought together a team of the world's best CGI artists. The artists had the chance to create an entire world of huge mountains, giant trees, and fantastical creatures. When audiences watched *Avatar*, they found it hard to believe that every part of Pandora had been created inside a computer!

The *Avatar* artists created the Na'vi race that inhabits Pandora.

Where It All Begins

So how do CGI artists bring to life the worlds and characters we love to see on the screen?

The CGI parts of a movie are created by artists who work for a VFX (Visual Effects) company. A team of artists includes concept artists, **modelers**, **riggers**, texture artists, and animators. It's possible to work in all these areas or specialize in just one.

Concept artists work with pencils, paint, and computer programs such as Photoshop and Painter.

The story for a movie is sometimes taken from a book. A concept artist carefully analyzes the author's descriptions of characters, places, and events to bring the book to life.

Concept artists are the first artists to work on a project. They might make hundreds of drawings or pieces of digital art to develop the movie's characters and scenery. Their work helps the rest of the team understand how the movie's world and characters will look. Once filming starts, they may need to redraw characters and places as the original ideas for the movie change.

To create their ideas, concept artists might research animals or real-life places, such as jungles, mountains, or historic buildings.

A movie storyboard

Before filming starts, storyboard artists draw the action. The storyboard is arranged in panels that show each scene **shot** by shot. This lets all the film crew know what will happen in each scene.

Making Models

The CGI work on a movie goes through a series of stages known as the pipeline. Once the concept artist's ideas are approved, the next stage in the pipeline is modeling.

An artist called a modeler takes the concept artist's ideas and creates a rough **3D (three-dimensional)** model on a computer, using modeling software. Next, using shapes called polygons, the artist creates a more detailed model on the computer.

The modeler might create people, animals, vehicles, a mountain, or a city street. In *The Day After Tomorrow*, New York City is flooded by a tsunami and then frozen under a thick layer of ice. The VFX team used 50,000 detailed photos of New York to create a realistic 3D digital model of the city.

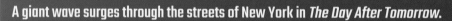

A giant wave surges through the streets of New York in *The Day After Tomorrow*.

New York is one of the best-known cities on Earth. The CGI artists knew they had to make their digital New York look 100 percent realistic!

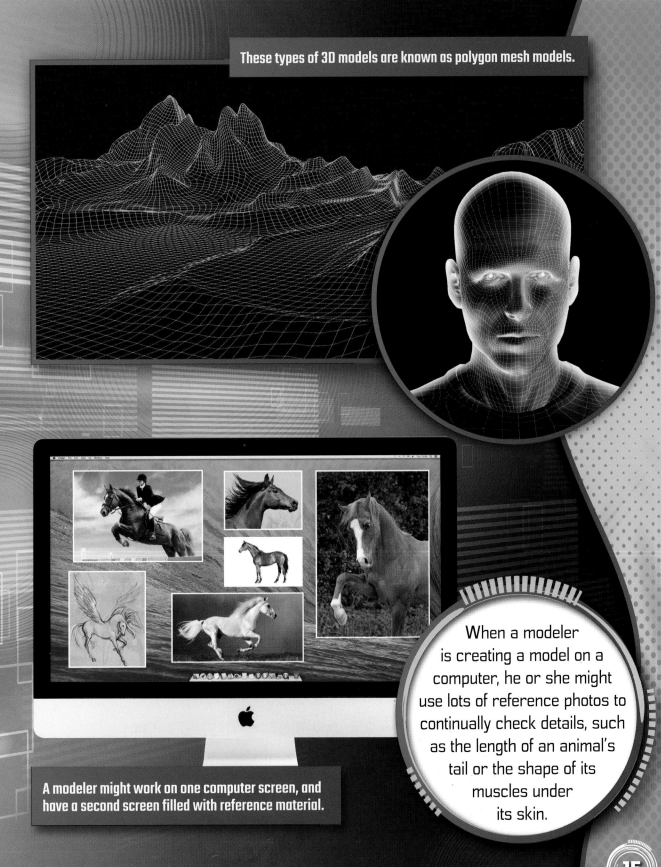

These types of 3D models are known as polygon mesh models.

A modeler might work on one computer screen, and have a second screen filled with reference material.

When a modeler is creating a model on a computer, he or she might use lots of reference photos to continually check details, such as the length of an animal's tail or the shape of its muscles under its skin.

The Texture Artists

When the modelers' work is completed, the texture artists take over. From fur to wrinkled skin, or brickwork to rusting metal, these artists add color and textures to the computer models of characters, buildings, and landscapes.

Texture artists use software programs to place photos of real-life textures onto models. Sometimes the texture they need, such as 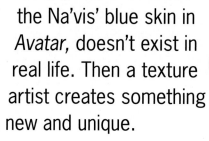 the Na'vis' blue skin in *Avatar,* doesn't exist in real life. Then a texture artist creates something new and unique.

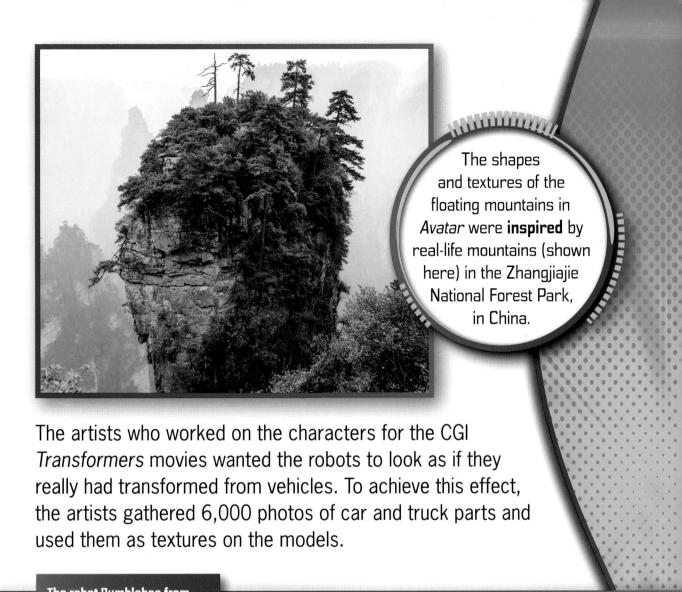

The shapes and textures of the floating mountains in *Avatar* were **inspired** by real-life mountains (shown here) in the Zhangjiajie National Forest Park, in China.

The artists who worked on the characters for the CGI *Transformers* movies wanted the robots to look as if they really had transformed from vehicles. To achieve this effect, the artists gathered 6,000 photos of car and truck parts and used them as textures on the models.

The robot Bumblebee from the 2011 movie *Transformers: Dark of the Moon.*

Bringing the Models to Life

Once a model—one of a character, for example—is complete, the next steps in the pipeline are to rig it and animate it in the computer.

Animating a model means to make it move. The job of a rigging artist is to give a model a digital skeleton. Each of the skeleton's joints is called a "handle" or control point. An animator clicks on the handles to make a model bend and move.

Animation is a very technical job. To make realistic animations, however, an artist must also be creative and pay lots of attention to detail.

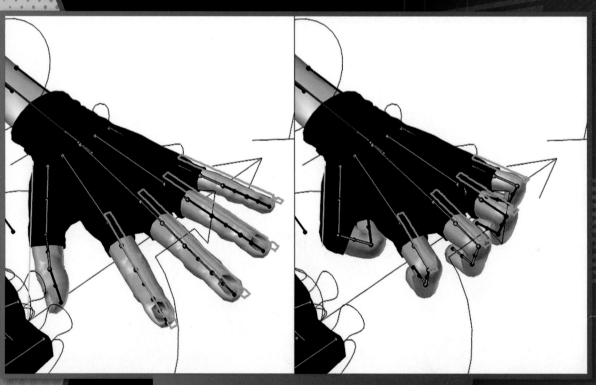

This image shows a rigged 3D model of a hand.
The bones are in green. The blue marks are the handles.

Using special software, animators can make a tiger pounce, a warrior fight, or even a torrent of water rush down a city street. Just a few seconds of on-screen action can take hours, or even days, of painstaking detailed work.

Fingers curling

Shirt bunching at hip

Shirt flapping to one side

Foot pointing backward

Many animators film themselves acting out movements. Then they watch for tiny details they can add to their animation to make it realistic.

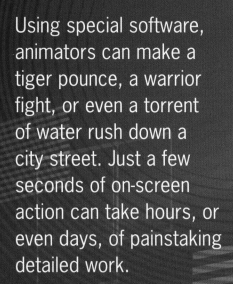

There are many things to think about to make an animation appear real. Even though this wolf is standing still, its sides will still rise and fall as it breathes, and its eyelids will blink.

Working with Motion Capture

Many animators make their characters move by using only animation software and their own skills. Another way to animate 3D characters is to use **motion capture**, which is sometimes called performance capture.

To animate with motion capture, an actor wears a suit that has markers on it. Cameras all around the set pick up signals from the markers. Then on a computer, the signals are used to create a moving skeleton of the actor that can drive, or move, the digital character.

Sometimes, facial motion capture is also used. Actors have tracking dots stuck to their faces. A high-speed camera on a helmet mount picks up signals from the dots and captures the actor's facial expressions in great detail. Then these expressions are applied to the CGI character's face.

Markers

Actors wearing motion-capture suits being filmed in a studio.

Andy Serkis (who plays the ape Caesar in *Dawn of the Planet of the Apes*) takes part in a live-action shot wearing a motion-capture suit.

Tracking dots

Helmet-mounted camera

To film motion capture, actors usually perform in a studio, often away from the main action. In *Dawn of the Planet of the Apes*, the filming of the motion-capture work was combined with the main live action— even outdoors.

The actors' motion-capture performances were used to animate the CGI apes.

Creating Gollum

Before there was CGI, the movie makers might put an actor in make-up and a bodysuit to produce a fantasy, human-like creature.

Today, characters such as Gollum, from the *Lord of the Rings* and *Hobbit* movies, are brought to life by CGI artists. Creating and animating humanoid characters and making them look real is not a simple task.

The CGI Gollum has been appearing in movies since 2001. Over the years, Gollum has become more and more realistic. To achieve this, CGI artists researched how skin and eyes react to light. They studied how real skin might slide over his scrawny muscles and bones. To create the effects they wanted, they had to develop new types of software.

Today when we watch Gollum on the screen, our heads tell us he isn't real. Our eyes, however, find that very hard to believe!

Advances in technology have enabled helmet-mounted cameras to capture increased detail in an actor's performance. Then performance-capture software applies the actor's emotions to a CGI character.

Sadness, anger, fear, surprise—using performance capture, all the human feelings shown by Andy Serkis (who plays Gollum) can appear on the little creature's face.

Back to the Jungle

Every second of *The Jungle Book* takes place in a jungle in India. The movie was filmed, however, in a studio in Los Angeles ... and then the CGI artists got to work!

The movie's artists gathered more than 100,000 photos of Indian jungles. They used this reference material to create vines, bark, moss on rocks—every detail.

Using CGI to produce a real-life environment was harder than creating a fantasy land like *Avatar*'s Pandora. Details such as sunlight filtering through trees or a character's shadow have to be realistic. We may not think about it much, but our brains know what the real world looks like. If the jungle looked fake, it would spoil the audience's enjoyment of the movie.

Some of the movie's animals were larger than real life compared to Mowgli. Director Jon Favreau wanted to create the feeling of what it's like to be a child in a big world.

The Bear Facts

As *The Jungle Book*'s CGI team worked on creating the movie's world, actor Neel Sethi was hard at work in a bare studio. Sometimes, he might have a log or rock to sit on. When he talked to his animal friends, he was often speaking to a crew member holding a puppet.

The scene where Mowgli floats along a river was filmed in a large tank of water—in a parking lot outside the studio. Director Jon Favreau climbed into the water so that Neel had someone to sing and chat to. Thanks to the movie's artists, what the audience sees in the final movie is a little boy splashing and floating in a jungle river with a large, friendly brown bear.

To understand how a bear might look floating in water, the CGI artists studied polar bears swimming in the ocean.

CGI characters from
The Jungle Book

It took a team of
around 800 CGI artists
to create *The Jungle Book*.
From modelers and texture
artists to riggers and animators,
the team's thousands of hours
of work made possible 105
minutes of magic.

Tomorrow's Movie Magic

Using technology, CGI artists can create realistic-looking wild animals and transport audiences to alien worlds. The men and women who work in CGI aren't just imaginative and creative. They are also technical wizards who use their skills to discover and invent new ways to use computer power.

Even today it's sometimes difficult to know what's real and what's CGI. How will it be 10 years from now? What technology will be available to CGI artists 20 years from now? If you are creative and love movies and computers, perhaps you could be one of tomorrow's top CGI artists.

What technology might you help invent? What will your audiences be watching? It's impossible to say. In fact, when it comes to CGI, there's probably only one certainty …

… nothing is impossible!

This CGI scene from *King Kong* is being filmed against a green screen.

Naomi Watts (who plays Ann Darrow) is looking at Andy Serkis (King Kong). Andy is positioned high above her so their eye contact looks realistic.

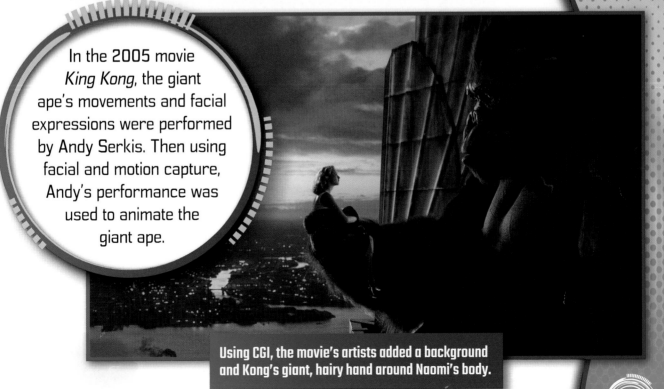

In the 2005 movie *King Kong*, the giant ape's movements and facial expressions were performed by Andy Serkis. Then using facial and motion capture, Andy's performance was used to animate the giant ape.

Using CGI, the movie's artists added a background and Kong's giant, hairy hand around Naomi's body.

Get to Work as a CGI Artist

Q&A

What skills does a CGI artist need?
You will need strong computer skills. Good art skills are also important for working as a concept artist or texture artist. You will need an eye for detail, good problem-solving skills, and lots of patience.

What subjects should I study?
Computer science and art. In college you can study art, computer science, and animation.

Where will I work?
You might work as part of a small or large team for a VFX company (often called a VFX house). Some jobs are permanent. Others last for the length of a project. You might work on a project for a few months. If it's a big-budget movie, such as *The Jungle Book*, you may work on the project for two or more years. If you're good, you might be asked back to work on a sequel!

When will I work?
If you're part of a big project and a deadline is approaching, be ready to work late at night and on weekends.

How soon can I get started?
Today! Sketch and work on character and scenery ideas. Look at the world around you with an artist's eyes, noticing details, such as the leaves on a tree or the way your dog or cat moves. Try creating your own animations with the Scratch online resources. (Follow the link on page 32.)

Create a Creature Concept

Get started on your career as a CGI artist today.
Can you create a totally new and unique fantasy creature?
You can illustrate your creature using pencils or paint,
or produce your work digitally.

When working on your ideas, think about these questions:

• What shape and size is your creature? Is it humanoid or more like an animal? Perhaps it's part machine, or something completely new and alien.

• How does it move? Study people, four-legged animals, birds, insects, spiders, or vehicles to watch how they move.

• What textures will you use for your creature? Does it have scales or feathers, or is it made from rusty metal or a made-up material that you've invented? Gather together reference pictures of animals or objects to create a library of textures to help you explain how your creature looks.

• Where does your creature live? What is its life story?

• What kind of character will your creature be in a movie? Is it a hero or an enemy?

The Demo Reel

CGI artists create a "demo reel" to show off their best work. A demo reel might be pieces of work on a DVD or website. Artists send their demo reels to VFX houses to try to get jobs. The work must be impressive, though, because a VFX company will receive hundreds of demo reels every month!

As a CGI artist you might also work creating video games. Concept artists, texture artists, modelers, riggers, and animators are all needed to create games.

Glossary

3D (three-dimensional)
(three-di-MEN-shu-nuhl)
Having or appearing to have height, width, and depth, rather than just something flat or two-dimensional.

animation (an-uh-MAY-shuhn)
A way of making drawings or computer-generated images appear to move.

animator (AN-uh-may-tur)
A person who makes drawings or computer-generated images move. In CGI, animators use computer software to animate images.

animatronic (an-uh-muh-TRON-ik)
Making a lifelike puppet or model move with electronics or pulleys and levers.

CGI (computer-generated imagery)
(kuhm-PYOO-tur-JEN-uh-rate-id IM-uh-jree)
Images that are created on a computer with different types of software.

frame (FRAME)
One of many still images that when combined create a piece of moving film.

groundbreaking (GROUND-brake-ing)
Being the first to do something; innovative.

inspired (in-SPIRED)
Given an idea of how to do something.

modeler (MAHD-lur)
A computer artist who uses modeling software to create 3D digital models, such as animals, vehicles, and landscapes.

motion capture
(MOH-shuhn CAP-chur)
An animation technique in which actors wear special suits that allow their movements to be captured and applied to a CGI character.

rigger (RIG-ur)
A computer artist who uses rigging software to create skeletons for digital models that will allow an animator to make the model move.

shot (SHOT)
The moment that a camera starts filming until the moment it stops. A movie may be made up of thousands of shots.

software (SAWFT-ware)
The programs that are used to operate computers.

studio (STOO-dee-oh)
A large building where movies and TV shows are filmed.

visual effects (VFX)
(VIZH-yoo-uhl uh-FEKTS)
Visual tricks that are used in movies and TV shows. Visual effects are created after all the normal filming is done, using miniature models or CGI.

Index

Read More

Anniss, Matthew. *Movie or TV Show (Create Your Own)*. Mankato, MN: Heinemann-Raintree (2017).

Way, Jennifer. *King Kong and Other Monstrous Apes (Greatest Movie Monsters)*. New York: Rosen Publishing (2016).

Learn More Online

To learn more about CGI artists and making movies, go to:
www.rubytuesdaybooks.com/CGI